like water to
STONE

like water to
STONE

A Collection of Poems By

STEVEN PELCMAN

Adelaide Books
New York/ Lisbon
2017

like water to STONE
A Collection of Poems
By Steven Pelcman

Copyright © 2017 By Steven Pelcman
Cover Image © 2017 Steven Pelcman

Published by Adelaide Books, New York / Lisbon
An imprint of the Istina Group DBA
adelaidebooks.org

Cover design & Interior Formatting:
Istina Group DBA, New York

Editor-in-Chief
Stevan V. Nikolic

For any information, please address Adelaide Books
at info@adelaidebooks.org

ISBN13: 978-0-9992148-9-3
ISBN10: 0-9992148-9-6

Printed in the United States of America

Dedicated to Mom, Dad and Bonnie

and to Jessica and Eric

*and to all those who have passed through
all the days of our lives*

*Special thanks to poet, teacher and mentor,
Dan Masterson.*

In the deep shadows
Still dark after they are gone
To share the warmth that color can give
Where the leaves darken
Against September's wind

Contents

Poems

A Dying Animal

Her paw weighs
no more than that
of a leaf and trembles
at even the sounds of light

that rise from under
the snow in winter,
and there is little more
to expect other than

a brief moment for her dying,
so that her whimpering
can melt away
under the heavy darkness.

I put my hand
in the bloody footprint
and feel moonlight
roll over me like fur

ruffling in wind
and I smell the odor
of something damp
and sticky and wild,

and I know that something
had been alive, that it had sung
the same song as darkness
sings to itself when no one is listening.

Steven Pelcman

A Hunter Waits

He waits in the cold
with schnapps and a twenty-two rifle
in a wooden look-out tower
on stilts overlooking a clearing,

now the thin winter ice,
as the moon's face slips across it,
hoping a wild pig or a hungry deer
will be suddenly caught by surprise.

Above the tree-line wine hills
with frozen dried out saps
still clinging to the vine
can feel the sifting wind

as it plucks its way through
the hedgerows.
He warms his body with alcohol
under the weight of the moon

as a deer slithers by
the thin dark trees gnawing
at bark and fallen leaves
and the shallow pools of water

the late winter night forms.
They look through the darkness
knowing that nothing protects them
but the warmth within.

A Bat Invades our Summer Bungalow

In late August when deer feel it is safe
to wander across Sullivan Road
and black bears sniff out
the last ripe berries

before September's chill
my mother airs out the bungalow
of stifling heat and wilted roses
first planted many summers ago.

She leaves open a window
and puts us to sleep
to the aroma of cold pine bark
and moss dripping wet in the moonlight

when it enters like a sudden awakening
to a nightmare and tumbles deep into itself;
a silhouette collecting darkness
as a wound discolors skin

to blanket the room with its wings.
Its madness drives my mother mad
with her one hand on top of her hair
in a bun while the other holds a broom

as the moon eavesdrops
against the wooden walls
and the sky thins into a faded blue
but this flying leech does not fly

and that's the thing that scares her most
as she watches it spread out its body
like a lost continent on a map
of white and yellow plastered walls

with its tiny eyes bulging and gritty teeth
fangs whiter than the kitchen lamp light
beaming light house signals
to sea creatures on the horizon.

She turns on all of the lights
and locks us in the bedroom
while she chases this sticky chunk of flesh,
its heart beating against one wall

then leaping to another turning my mother
into a housewife Don Quixote with a broom
muttering words like a lost tongue
only she and it would understand.

They danced this way in the cold summer air,
she afraid it would nest in her hair
and it afraid the stars would not show the way
to the endless darkness it longed for.

A Gathering

The night in winter
does not roll in lazily.
Instead it bursts over the city

like a dark wound
spreading quickly.
There is a park we pass

on the way into the city
near an old Russian church
off of Tulla street

where old men huddle
over a small fire.
Their shadows press tightly

like a clump of trees
listening to the darkness
chanting a prayer lost

in the wind
only the dying
would remember.

They are not alone
as black birds
like mobsters

stalk the snowy field
burying their own shadows
into the hard ground.

They congregate like rigs
on a Texas oil field
exploiting the earth

with their beaks
until the moon
is a piece of gold

hurtling before them
but they do not fly away,
they leap and stretch

their necks out as if drunk
on cold air, and the men
join in by stomping

to keep their feet warm
and clapping their hands
to shake off the chill.

This is the dance
of the forgotten
that silently migrate

and know no difference
between day or night.
One by one they leave

and drift away
to the sound of church bells
that echo against the darkness.

A Walk with Miguel

Miguel tells us
that what is buried here
stays here,
under the Portuguese sun
as he fans himself
with the straw hat

he swings by his side,
and that when we see
petals fall and the last bees
hover as awkward heads
of raw-green skin
suddenly appear

that that is when
apples bud and dangle
like unwanted words
and then blossom
tilting this way and that.
This he tells us

means that spring has arrived
as the newborn sunlight
leans against the slope
above a small stream
flowing through the valley
where cork oak trees

in open woodlands
are warm to the touch
in the sheer wind passing
as nearby sheep graze
and Iberian pigs
thrive on the fallen acorns.

Miguel's hobbled walk
is steady like an old horse
put out to pasture
and against the blinding sunlight
he is more scarecrow than man
but we keep up

stride for stride
past the slanted hillside-
fincas and eucalyptus ready
for the harvest
and the olives
recently picked;

the marks of nets
dried in the ground
where the shaken olives
had fallen and are kept
beside the stone walls
in barrels.

Miguel says it is better
to be here now
rather than in the dry heat
of summer when crickets
sing and the vines
are weighed down by fruit

and when buses full of tourists
roam the old mosaic floors
entombed in foundations
lived over for thousands of years
he says, antiquity like all else
is best kept in the dark.

He is an old man
who is careful with his smile
and as careful at picking bones
from sardines and tipping
his hat to old woman passing
on their way to market.

He has lived here forever
he says as do
his ten grandchildren
he reminds us
when he extends his hand
for the coins and dollars

we lay flat on his tanned palm
and as we head back
to the parked car beside the café
with a shiny apple and green olives
still full of grass we had taken
from the fields,

Miguel is approaching another couple
talking aloud of Roman ruins,
of hillsides full of olives and sheep,
of acorns and the smell of spring,
of how an old man with ten grandchildren
knows the secrets of old Rome.

He Needed to Know
(For Daniel)

She had refused to lie still
and speechless having promised
her children that death
need not be boring and sad

but the tubes and morphine
weighed heavily against her
moist pajama and her son
would not let her go.

They shared the same dark room
and smelled the medicine and counted
breaths together taking them back
to when they had both been young

and he remembered how to be patient
without the frustration he had often shown
as a small boy trying to understand why
his mother had not loved him.

The cool early spring air
at the lake where they lived
jabbed at her like doctors
and the forlorn words

they used when they took her off
chemo, that her body rejected,
so they sent her home
to gaze at waves

whose purpose is only
to reach the shore
and retract within themselves.
This summer he will sit alone

counting the white sails
skirting beneath
the moon's crest,
the sun burning

the edges of sky
until its face turns pale
and relaxes its muscles
into a fragile darkness.

This summer he will sit at the shore
and recall how she had taught him
to swim and dive and to hold
his breath under water

and how his sudden absence
beneath the rippled waves
had not changed
the warmth of the sun.

Key Largo

("One by one, 3 utility workers
descended into a manhole.
One by one, they died.")

On Long Key Road
the smell of rotten eggs
drew three utility workers
to an endless truth

without veering from the
tropical sunlight surrounded
by woody shrubs
and hardwood trees

they followed their shadows
familiar to the patterns of one another;
each stride as correct
as the next,

each habit repeated
in an understood silence
having measured
their distance before

understanding the animal twitches
and the trust they shared
and the relief each one
depended on.

They followed the music
of who they are
when they removed
a manhole cover

breathed in the decomposed
vegetation and descended
into the earth
in the same soldierly manner

whenever they had found themselves
in danger no matter the season
the sun falls beyond the horizon
anointing each wave

before it slips out of sight
leaving its memory to linger
as men do to carry on
after they are gone.

This began thousands of years
ago in an eternal image
of each man rising
unwilling to fall

learning to be a man
learning to love something
bigger and distinguish themselves
to survive.

There is nothing subtle in this
yet they feel the warmth
of each stoic stare
and sculptured grin

on the hot pavement
of a neighborhood by the sea
one man opens the passageway
to the earth's underbelly

and like every man before him
I have seen, once a man landing
on the moon, a miner stalking
the earth with a pick and shovel

a soldier's hastily built foxhole
to sink into the depth's darkness,
what else was he to do
but to lower himself

into the unknown
so one by one after the silence
of one man another descended
only to share the same secret

of eternity and be overcome
by poisonous fumes
that lie beneath Monroe County;
a hole below just wide enough

to fit a man's body was
filled with hydrogen sulfide
and methane gas created
from years of rotted vegetation;

a little town like any other
by the sea where once I heard
a thousand sounds drowned out
by the silence of the sun.

Ireland

All day the salty air
flutters like wings
shedding light

across the flat bristled land,
the scrubby mounds
so green they turn black.

A skulking fox, matted fur,
damp in the Irish wind
where once bears snouted

their way across
the grassy knolls.
Shadows find shelter

in a creviced slope
that curves towards the sea
as the sun slips

behind a jagged cliff
where a dirt road
ends in darkness.

The marshes turn blue
as the last wave
rushes ashore.

What secrets lie tucked
beneath ancient stones,
what hidden footprint

tells a forgotten story,
whose bones lie buried
under the shallow pools,

how many frozen breaths
protect the first flowers
of spring.

The Widow Maker

She did not think
that the small purple
mark on the back
of her knee
would turn into

a long black stripe,
an evil shadow
deeply etched
and unwilling
to disappear.

The garden she had been
playing in let her swim
her hands through
the weeds
covering her knees

and like any other animal
would, hoping to find
food or spring at butterflies
or bees mapping out
the airy space.

In the near dirt where
the grass is flat and flimsy,
a cluster of tiny legs and heads
are swaying in a cradle
of blackness waiting

for a mother known
to devour her mates
leaving tiny punctures
on a young girl
burning up in fever.

The black widow spider
rolled its head
and wrapped its legs
to steal a secret kiss
of venom into the tight-white skin

of a little girl comparing
the height of flowers
growing out of her clenched
fist only to see
the short hairs

on the last segment
of a fourth pair of legs
which are used to wrap
their prey in silk
and cuddle to death.

Taos Pueblo
(New Mexico pueblo, abandoned.
Tourists $10.00 per entry per person)

As old women shiver on the open plain
with buckets of water and wood
for kivas to send pinion-wood smoke
blowing through sage and high desert mesa,

you can press your ear
against a low moon
settling on the snowy foothills of Sangre de Cristo;
and hear dangling corn twirling

in the wind, whistling
through horse and cow skulls,
mud and straw
and over the cemetery's white crosses

past a few old men straddling
a fence smoking tobacco
and waiting for winter.

Even though it is now
perfectly dark
you can feel their slouched shoulders
take on the mountain's imperfections

and sense how the darkness
once filled everything
with the weight of wild horses.

Steven Pelcman

The Stranger at 3 AM
(A father with Alzheimer's)

I know that it is you
because I can smell your age
behind the closed door
and hear your shuffling feet

go back and forth
between our bedrooms,
a distance you cannot measure
in the dark.

And so you stand there
gasping for the slender
light that reaches you
from under my door,

and we both knew
you came to tell me
you were dying again,
that you were living out
someone else's life
that you were greedy
for every last drop of light,

that you were too afraid
to feel safe
and that in not knowing
what to do
you knew to stand there
softly breathing against the wood
practicing to be noticed.

Lake Shrine
(Buddhist meditation temple in Los Angeles)

The prayers stop,
and chanting blows
the stillness
across the lake

where one young woman
whose lines are more
than poetry, sits alone
beneath trees
where the leaves darken

and hide the struggle
of one child, in a wheelchair,
bound and gagged
by back and neck braces
shaking violently
to free himself, like an animal
caught in a private moment.

Limp bodies pose
against a lake's stone wall
with a single focus
on white swans
passing between trees
and ducks wind-milling
their feathers into small disturbances
of tiny ripples carrying sunlight.

Goodbye

When you think of them
you remember their voices.

Hers was full of light.
It curled its way into you
the way a cat unravels itself
nudging you with tenderness.

His was a forest
whispering beneath the wind
deriving a melody from within
that brushed aside the darkness.

Their voices spoke
and touched you
coming closer the way shadows
replace sunlight
when each time
becomes the first time.

And as we stood
holding hands in a circle
it is what we remembered
as we threw sand
and little pebbles
into the freshly dug ground.

A Small World

My mother and I
walk leaf-quiet,
her hands as delicate
as birds as we pick berries

from a blue spot of grass
rising with heat
in its summer madness of bees.
Her garden roses open innocently

to the fractured light
to not threaten a butterfly
carefully lifting its wings
to worship in this temple

of imagined seashells
sharing whispers
in the remaining shade.
How alike they are

the butterfly, a buoy
guarding the open sea,
each rose, a dying breath
sweetly awaiting the darkness

like mother, younger than trees then
and in the moonlight when I dream
back, her fingernails
move softly as petals.

Pool

Trauma creates its habits;
odd comfort zones
we come to rely on
and so the day
my sister almost died

I was hypnotized and shaking
wet as water sloshed about
against the sides of the swimming pool
that had seen her body
fished out by someone else's father.

One minute she had been
a lily pad shimmering white
over something glossy and perfect
and the next moment
found her back scaled

and bony filling
with air making her ribs
ride a wave
that ran inside of her
and I thought it was

a miracle, the kind
we dream of and that heaven
was still water and dragon flies
gently landing in fluttering
pockets of sunlight.

My sister had known everything then;
what it was like to be afraid
and need love and I was jealous
of the near death I had missed out on
being only a bystander

watching air bubbles
become grey pearls
popping out of her mouth
as her black hair swept over her
like darkness draping a coffin.

I sat by her, listening
to the wind as her angry body
changed into forgiveness.
I had always known
mother loved her best.

Andrej

Walking into the spring light
and out of the shadows
he left behind
to stand by the fire
made him a believer

in the dark secrets
grandma told him
he would understand in time.
And so he became grandpa's
first responder;

the little helper
who inched his way
closer to the rising magic
of a barbecue flame
turning black coal

as white as sunlight.
He masked his face
against the smoke
with his tiny palm
and squeezed his eyes

half-closed and froze
in the burning glare
the way forest animals do
until grandma assured him
that the bucket of water

grandpa keeps nearby
will save them
and keep them safe
the way his fingers feel
in grandma's hand.

Thinking

All night long
I pretend the rising moon
is just another curious face
studying me from a distance

until clouds like creatures
crawling through sand
breach a rift and out pours
blue smoke into a haze

where a single boatman
drifts as if dark trout
beneath a shallow sea
lead him away.

Leaning against the window
where time is measured
in the flapping of wings
that blink their way across

the skies, darkness
no longer separates
but rather binds me
to every moving star

and I think that nothing good
can come from all this thinking
that a mass of blackness
cannot be without reason

and that perhaps it is the last
breath of the dying
that robs us of sunlight
each night.

Blind

They walked out of the snow
with slouched backs into the tram,
literally; the blind leading the blind,
a gentle tapping
pointing out their way,
and sat down next to each other

their backs tipping over and their canes
alongside their outstretched legs,
and as they sat finding comfort
easily by touch and sound
their distance to other passengers
was felt in a calm hunger

for knowing where they were
as if their eyelids, like the horizon
understood distance and shape
but could not be pressed further
than beyond that end
to which their probing hands

only reached for each other
not for help, but for play
as their bodies enjoyed
the movement, enjoyed
the expected juggling about
and then laughed and she

came closer to kiss
his closed eyes
knowing that darkness
does not always erase
memories and that memory
is never better than imagination.

Steven Pelcman

Bee in Classroom

It enters from
a window in the rear
caught in its tumbling
yellow and looking
for some sense of green.

Lost in a room of
bent walls and old paint
it skips from desk
to desk its wings electric
and whining

as a part of regular chatter
then circles for prey
to land on, disturbed
and curious of the desolation
and blandness it is trapped in.

Finally, it settles
on a windowsill nudged
against a familiar light
exhausted by its own urges
and stumbles the length

of cracked glass
till an opening is found
where its swirling body
loses color
and slips away.

Between the Lost
and the Forgotten

The night comes
and someone always goes with it
as he shuffles by
dressed in only a diaper
unsure of where the bedroom is.

His hands know the music
of small things
as he walks, almost enchantingly,
on a pure white floor
full of a wife's discipline.

He travels in circles thinking
that his is a little death
the dark will not grieve over
and tightens his face
as insects do to unknown sound.

He does not belong
to the silence yet
and goes on imagining
where a straight line
can take him.

Left Behind

Untamed silhouettes guide the rowboat
forward beside the rising sun
slowly diluting the black sea
and expanding the distance to shore.

A narrow lip
of moonlight stricken full of
smudges against the flat sky
gives life

to the pole
the old man dips
into the moving water
as he has done every day of his life.

His timing is everything
fish seem to know in advance
and think of it as a kindness
below the surface

where the measure of the man
is lost against the dead light
that finds his stiffened back
rowing to keep pace.

Light is no friend
he says, "It scares the fish away.
It is the darkness that brings life
to the soul".

Often, I wonder about that rowboat,
bobbing empty, other than for the
smell of the man pouring out of
the rotting wood that makes me

see him clearly through the
eyes of fish still clearing a path
in the blindness of deep waters
and the darkness he has left behind.

Steven Pelcman

The Day Grandfather Died

Six and alone but for an army
of voiceless dancing ballerinas,
bears and clowns stuffed and
lined up at edge of the bed,

she could not understand why
their pale and red cheeked faces
shined in the dim light or why
they refused to cry or blink or grin

no matter how often
her parents had screamed.
She placed her hands over Teddy's ears,
so he did not hear and she swore him

to secrecy so that he could not tell,
not even grandpa who never shouted,
whose wrinkled hands had held her
lovingly as their noses touched

and smiling eyes playfully
rolled hours before
and who now lies still
in the other room;

his black beaded eyes staring
into nowhere; his body swallowing
the same empty sound
sunlight makes as it fades away.

Acceptance
(For Donall)

His frail body rises and saunters
to the sounds of Irish wind
over the bog stumbling at 4AM
without a care in the dark

to the bathroom
with a thankful lingering sigh
and whiskey-mumbling lips
still clinging to the last round.

He clears his throat
as if rehearsing for a final song
and returns to the dark
hallway and the stale smell

of his pipe that guides him
to the right room,
to where his wife had belonged,
to where her outline remains

but it is the unexpected prayers
afterwards that breach
the joint bedroom wall
and take even the darkness

by surprise and yet
how alike they are,
still, alone, godly patient
for the first single thread of light.

The Young Wife

She has lived the last year
with the scent of death
walking her husband at 23
to the bathroom
shaving his face

watching him sit on the toilet
holding onto flimsy paper
as a child holds onto
a security blanket
afraid in the dark

then taking his stooped body
wrapped in blue terrycloth
back to bed
his frail fingers
picking at loose threads
with the confused ease
of children pulling wilted flowers
in a forgotten field.

In runs her three-year-old son
searching for his reflection
in daddy's colorless eyes

and all the while
from the bedroom's hidden corner
she rubs her own thighs
with fingers that sneak away
from the dying
to vacation on layers of skin
only he would have known

and as she takes out his shirt
to wear and rub
his old sweat against her breasts,
remembers how easy it was
to be a wife.

Sugar
(Remembering Sarajevo April 6, 1992)
(For Alemka)

We pass a café in the mist
and watch a hand as silky
as swans stretching to be seen
in the last water reflection,

silently unwrapping a sugar cube
as if a secret from its white coat.
She gingerly launches it and watches
it float above the dark steam.

It floated like petals and then sank
into a bed of dreams,
as the night closes down
around us while the woman sips

coffee in the Paris rain.
It was then that you tell me
at university you had collected
sugar cubes from cafes

and stored them in a box and that
you had never collected a duplicate
making sure they were different
and that the bold letters of café names

were alphabetized and arranged
by dates. You could not travel then,
not with bombs falling on Sarajevo,
you said, the fear of not knowing

what would happen every evening
made a cup of coffee feel like Paris
in the rain and in the dark;
it tasted so sweet.

Saturday Morning at Market Square
(Karlsruhe, Germany)

Dark-skinned and poor,
she mumbles out prayers
as her wide back stretches over
her scarred knees

and her dirty fingers turn into
rubbery tentacles crawling against
the cold pavement
begging for money.

She is colorless and frozen,
moulded and shaped
out of grey marble
befriended by only pigeons

nudging pebbles and bread crumbs
into the February morning light.
The black Burqa leaves nothing
but her eyes as dead as winter

lost in the careless movement
of people passing
so that the little child
whose shivering body

nesting in her lap
goes almost unnoticed
having learned to not cry
louder than street noise.

Jessica
(A father's last visit
with his ten-year old daughter)

I left you to nibble
at the root of spring
in the yard where we counted
Blue birds grieving
over misplaced shapes
and tree stumps freshly cut.

Taking pictures with careful smiles
on red bricks glued in moss
a black sky
turned us into shadows and
like leaves against the wall,
you came closer to find warmth.

I think of you
in that little corner tucked away
in banana trees and palm
rolling your eyes
at the edge of the sun
before the darkness
defined us.

Herbie

(YARMOUTH, Maine-AP – Herbie, a massive tree that stretched 110 feet into the sky, captured the imagination of a town's residents and earned the title of New England's champion elm, was cut down Tuesday after a long battle with Dutch elm disease. It was more than 200 years old.)

Herbie has stretched itself
above the shores of Yarmouth
for 200 years and never learned
to count the yellowing leaves

or dark streaks
it wore as the circling
of bark beetles
turned this old elm

inward over to the terror
of machines that know
no kindness
or remember the history

of fallen branches-
hallow thuds upon the wet earth
and escaping ghosts
that echo the silence

of this forest in dismembered limbs
that tumble and roll
across the snowy-mud
and dormant leaves of winter.

Better yet
to feel the shortness of breath
of townspeople witnessing
this scalping of this sticky wood

and splintered past
of men and horses passing
of rifle shot and young
lovers and lost graves

where children and families
have come to measure out
their lives in sliced
rings of wood.

Saving Frogs

In clumps of grass
where green struggles

against September's wind
my daughter circles to search
the thickest part, for legs, beady eyes

and humpback skin
and follows frog sounds
that slurp through a drainpipe ravine.
She is saving frogs
she says, parallel dancing

crisscrossing the stream
ahead, behind each sound
every air bubble that rises
to the surface, holding a glass jar
with white rocks and silky water,

twig poked holes
in silver foil paper tops.
And when one is caught,
she is encircled by other children
panting from the run across fields

with sacrificial flies in their fists.
Huddled about they shake
as each heart beat and gulp oozes
between her palm and thumb.
In the late afternoon

kept safe as a trophy in glass and
forgotten on a porch for hours,
only marigolds now full of twilight
survive the heat.
At night she creeps barefoot

and alone in the dark,
stares at the frog's black-purple seed eyes,
lifts the jar like a test tube
as if expecting
something to grow.

Summer Love

Which animals have grazed
in the safety of night
or children turning over sod
and small boulders discovering
worms traveling in circles
or old men and women
paying homage to first love
I do not know,

but it was enough
to watch the wind trace
your outline against tree shadows
to make me fall in love
in the middle
of this Sunday patch
as your shape takes hold
and softens the hard ground.

Your body, not yet summered
makes grass greener,
and lies beneath an unseen downpour
of tumbling petals
where tulips, born teardrops
under the earth, burst free
and lust the midday sun
as their silent voices of color

rise up, bloom
across foot-trodden
dirt mounds thick
of wild daisies
whispering first breaths.
Here, I am caught up
in the scent of you,
a stranger amongst the leaves.

Steven Pelcman

Mont-Saint-Michel
(Normandy, France)

The sun fades
and dips over
the fortress walls
and slowly blackens

everything and everyone
into a collection
of dark leaves
groping for the moonlight.

You would have been happy
to be a salt-meadow lamb
grazing on the grasses
of this bay watching

the dying sunlight
immortalize every step and stone.
You would have stood
at the ramparts

touching the granite
looking out across the bay
when the sea recedes
and the shimmering mud

of sand spills out
of an open fist.

It surrounds the monastery
until the dark waters
fill up again
into a deep silence

erasing every trace
of life.

If you could
you would have been
a visiting pilgrim waiting to see
a monk forested in wool

among the tourists
and counting the cobbled steps
as the moon's face
rises above them.

But what you said
you had wanted most
was to watch painters
smudge paint on canvass

and clench brushes
in their mouths
the way birds carry
off food or twigs

for shelter
to hold back
the tiny screams
of color they cry out.

Falling

She looked up
counting the first snow flurries
twirling, some crumbling
across the blackness

thinking they could be permanent
if you could only count them
before they landed
and dissolved.

They fell the way she and
her friends fall;
light-hearted and clumsy,
the earth swept away

under their feet
like ballerinas
spinning in a dream
but instead she opened her mouth

and felt the wetness press against
her lips to make them shine,
and said "there, the flakes now live
inside me" thinking she too

could learn to fall forever
and never have to
touch the earth again,
to count and count

and swallow whole
the darkness
and dance in the air
for all time.

First Moment of Custody Visit
(For Eric)

From turtle flesh to child
in a cartoon's moment at the age of five
he is tender as raindrops
evil as a lost sock.

His fingers trace
my tree-ringed eyes traveling
the broken pavement.

We hug,
I search for memories
in his brown tumbleweed hair
and blue-grey moon eyes.

Gently, he breathes against my chest;
a child's warm air misting,
like a store front window
in the cold.

Home

Beneath these hills
steeples rise above
the imagination of color.

I long for the rocks of Ireland
swept over by the sea,
for the scattered tufts

of green grass
and small trees among
the wild pastures

and for the carved earth
hedged and lined
like the age of a man's face.

I feel the pain of stories
told in the eyes of wandering sheep
and beside white cliffs

I long to put my ear
to the ground
and hear the songs

of whales and the bells of goats
and feel the salt
in the maddening wind.

Buying a Rug at the Istanbul Bazaar

She never imagined herself sitting
on a Turkish carpet in a box-of-a-store
of rugs and carpets bunker-high piled

to the ceiling, drinking tea and watching
the water-pipe smoke hover and spy
on her every thought.

She haggled over the price,
though buying a rug
is not about money,

while the picture of her body wrapped in silk
and wool opening up at night
mingled with the scent of apple and black tea.

From grandmother to mother their rugs
bore witness and covered the wooden floors
with warmth on the dark nights

of a Balkan winter as the steamy vapors
of black tea were poured
into tulip shaped glasses.

From grandmother to mother to daughter
to Turkish tea drunk on rugs
reflecting a language of its own

in the lives of women born to women
born to the stitched hand-woven knots,
born to the deep-throated bray of donkeys

and nomads of the high desert mountains
alive in the melodies of rugs lying flat
against the world singing its prayers and pain.

Now she sits in a dark corner
remembering the stories
of how her grandmother had walked over

the stitched flowers screaming of color,
then kneeling in prayer with the sun rising
 awakening the gentle touch of god in her voice.

Acroterion

They lean into your world
from a façade with a different sense
having been chiseled in an age
of fine distinct lines with serious mouths
and brooding eyes

and are the keepers of cobblestone,
narrowed and angled streets
like rivers and tributaries spreading
through and around cities.
And above us

on buildings adorned
and pastoral, admired and forgotten,
these heads of Europe, these angels
and bloody battle scenes;
their lives passing

like turned pages of history;
generations of stone discolored
and worn now rubbing shoulders
with the baker and pizza maker
and student who gives them no thought.

He-gave you world philosophy,
she-lost her head, they-redefined faith,
he-created symphonies
and poems alive forever;
sins remembered and discovered,

lands conquered and full of bone and blood,
science scorned and ships sailing the seas
and so it is easy to feel the solid steel
of a sword and march down the old streets
and feel the weight of time.

Steven Pelcman

KwaZulu-Natal, South Africa

What is left on the other side
of the moon rises
like a black noise twittering
under a soft black rim.
Everything is in motion.

Everything moves farther away.
Every breath is heard.
It is dark blood filling the air.
And the earth mourns. This is Africa
buried under the music

of shuffling feet.
Girls carry baskets on their heads
as children clinging
to their legs and arms
swing freely

past stalls of monkey oranges
and wooden carvings
and handmade dolls,
past women in billowing skirts
with red ochre thickly smeared.

over their bodies and long hair
making them prehistoric
and as empty as lions resting
under Mopane trees or as ungainly
as giraffes mating in the bush.

Each operatic moment
is filled with the movement
of people and herds
of wildness passing
mud and straw huts

and tiny sheds
made of timber planks
that glow in the morning fires
like worms feeding
off of the sunlight.

We sit as still as shadows
waiting for the drum beat
that reaches across the pan
to sear the jungle heart
and leave us with nightmares.

Steven Pelcman

An Impression

Reduced to a shadowy figure
pressed against sunlight
like smudges of paint,
she is cloaked in white clouds
which frame her,
and wears the changing sunlight

in her long dress
hemmed in wild flowers
and a flowing scarf
as if a part of the blue sky
was wind-blown around her neck.
She searches the horizon

while her skin
absorbs the scent of the sea
and she turns to the left
as Monet had imagined
she would.
At the edge of a bluff

her silhouette
beckons for the white sails
adrift to enter her narrow vision
which every sailor
hungers for at the end
of every journey.

Mountain Lake in Fall

Is it any wonder
that when sheep drink
out of these geese waters
they dream of flying
over this mountain lake

guarded by stalks of corn
posing in green sunlight.
Like drunken sailors
we trolled
the circled dirt path

like satellites spinning
to an end and then
she ran across the short grass
and plunged naked
amongst the feather flapping

and sunken white bellies,
the suspicious eyes
and nervous beaks
garbling out mouthfuls
of sheep lullabies.

How I wish
I could have grown wings
and hugged her
with the shaggy warmth
of darkness.

At the Window

The old woman stares
out perching her weight
against the sill and perhaps
sees what I do not.

The cold air of fall
makes her grimace
as her body crunches
and folds together to keep

the warmth safe.
She does not flinch
as birds pass and sunlight
filters its way

through the dirty glass
nor does she change position
to the sounds that come
from the street.

Like an outline drawn
at a crime scene
there is both emptiness
and memory looking

straight out at the sickly sky
making her a witness
to something hidden,
to something she is afraid

to let go of.
My mother once stood
at the foot of the bed
where my grandfather

lay covered in a white sheet.
A sheet as deep and as full
as any cloud could be.
She too

did not move
and only stared down
and across him
as if some hill to climb.

Silence

The young man
has a hard time of it;
pushing the gurney along
the outdoor walkway
of a building that shrinks
against the growing shadows.

The body enshrined
in its dark movement
cooperates more than
the narrow space
to the elevator,
and out it comes

into the silence
of the changing light.
Was this his first time
I wonder
because his triumphant shoulders
make me turn away

only to see my father
in the distance
walking towards me
when the body
is crammed into the ambulance.
Father did not see the

spinning red lights
of the fire rescue truck
and must have thought,
later at night
in his bedroom,
that it had been the mailman.

He undresses with the memory
of a wife taking off
his ring and watch
and tucking them neatly
into a box that once played
music when he had opened it.

Steven Pelcman

Adirondack Mountain Lakes
(Fall day)

I come here
to listen to the cackle
of the loon

and see it pummel
the lake water
beside moose antlers in the mist

then splash with the forest humor
of a twisting fish
in its beak.

The moon becomes faceless
and retreats into the milky sleep
of an infant's eye

and watches the sun
rise
all day.

No greater magic than darkness
could catch the opal crystals
of sunlight through the blue haze

finding dark timber
speechless
and leaves

falling to the ground
bound as lovers
sharing deep secrets.

Room 229

She returns from surgery
not knowing that fear
would smell like left-over food
and rubbing alcohol vapors
would seep out of the window
left ajar to almost
purify the heavy air
or that a wash cloth
could provoke such tenderness
as to return color
to her pale face
the way dusk light
for a moment
illuminates everything
that rises from the earth.

Station M8

Even from the waiting room
where medicinal air
filters throughout,
the windows buckle
at the sounds of helicopter blades

sauntering between buildings
forcing tree leaves to rain
upon the dry cement patio
at the hospital entrance.

We wait
on a three-seated black couch
rife with arterial tributaries
showing age
in their white-scarred lines

as nurses scurry by
with fixed smiles
and pockets bulging
of cell phones.

Other patients return
like unwanted mail
delivered to their rooms
when we last see her
under a thick-white blanket

rolled on a bed
in and out
of hallway shadows
towards the elevator

departing like so many departures
we have come to know
where waiting in line
or on planes, as bridesmaids,
and "dead men walking"

or the unemployed
who fear
the anticipation and expectations
of the unknown.

Deer Frozen in Headlights
(Highway 1 California to Oregon)

Would you believe me
if I told you his eye
was large and muddied
by a lingering winter?

And if I told you
its eye was large enough
to hold the rising sun
or a cool moon
as they rotated
beneath and above him
while he stood still,
would you believe me then?

Could you imagine,
as I did,
that an eye
could fill up
with waves crashing out
the high-pitched throaty sounds
of migrating whales
and still feel the shifting
of weight upon
a single leaf?

How is it
that a dark circle
can pull out secrets
we keep to ourselves,
remind us of our loneliness,
make us live out
our pain and wonder
if the earth moves as we see it,
and still feel the tenderness
of its quiet beauty?

He stands alone
against the forest shadows
just outside that tangled isolation,
that sullen world
free of understanding;
nothing escapes,
nothing is forgotten.

You know this;
to look deeply into anything
for time passes slowly
in everything we see
and what we remember
we remember forever.

Tuscany

From atop the hillside
the Valdiciana below
wears a mask of darkness
in September

as she settles onto
his shoulder
the way young Etruscan lovers
may have once met

at the stone wall
of Cortona,
and her face nests
in his open hand

as if reborn and together
they grow larger
than the withdrawing light
of a reluctant sun.

She is paper-thin
and the air,
chocolate-sweet
as a cool breeze

sweeps its way
along the narrow streets
to wrap around
the golden hue

crowning olive trees
and cypresses
and the little farmhouses
just beyond reach.

They hold hands
and walk away
as if from the distant thunder
of Roman armies

outside the city gates
still marching
in the shadows
above the valley.

Steven Pelcman

The Last Morning

Cheryl's father sits
on the little porch
they had especially built

and attached to the mobile home
which is far enough away
yet still close by the main house

making him as much as family
as Henry, the lone gelding
circling the corral.

Henry is crunching the peanut hay,
its ears twitching at horse flies
on the open field.

The old man sees his image shaking
in Henry's deep-sunken
black eyes turning red

with the rising sun.
He has given up
counting in people years

adopting a horse's life
of solitude but without
the bulging muscle

and the head-tossing
stubbornness of his own
youth when he had roamed freely.

His weathered hands
match the corral
dripping with the dew

of an early Florida morning
as the sun rays
almost snap open

the tall stand
of trees at the far
edge of the property.

He has come to understand
the pouring out
of wildness on the land

in the stomping rhythm
of horse beats he matches
as he taps

against the wooden boards
with his right boot
still muddied and torn.

They are not so different
man and horse in the aging of flesh
or in the dreams

they may share
or in the music
of the night grass

that beckons under
the muted moonlight
that frightens them.

Steven Pelcman

Sunday's Visit with Mom

I took my little son
to a gravesite where
his mother lies in stone
and he put his hand

across the surface
and spread out
his tiny fingers apart
listening for her voice

and said he had never
heard her so angry before,
as the wind tossed leaves
still wet from the night rain.

He then placed his hand
in the nearby sand
full of a spot
where nothing seemed to grow

and spread out his fingers again
and oddly smiled,
saying everything was okay now
because the sand made her

feel warm, and the wind stopped blowing
as my son leaped into my arms
and put his hand on my face
and I swear, I could hear her too.

Family Diary
The Farm 1919

Part 1
Sunday night March 9

The low light makes it hard
to write these words
and the swell of wind
across the prairie
keeps thumping

against the windows
that I can hardly think
but I can hear him
beneath me as poppa shuffles
from room to room so

that I can almost hum
a song to his rhythm
and picture his swollen hands
those same hands
that had just gently

prepared sandwiches and hot tea
with whiskey for momma
as she sat on her chair
rocking herself to sleep
beside the fire.

And I would watch him
take his night stiffness
and cover momma
with a blanket
blowing out kitchen candles

leaving the last part of him
on frozen windows.
I hear the shuffling in my sleep
and hum tunes into my pillow
to the spinning

of rusted wagon wheel spokes.
Poppa would be forever
mending crooked nails
in dry wood and buildings
leaning as trees into wind

that carries my grandfather's laughter,
my little sister's Jen's high voice,
the howling of wolves.

Family Diary
The Farm 1919

Part 2
Tuesday night March 25

The tall grass
and wild flowers
whisper at night
and the quiet purr
of windswept Minnesota with rain

shines in the moonlight
competing with
grandfather's warm knees
little Jen sit on
learning to count

by buttoning and unbuttoning
his shirt
and momma's quiet gestures
along Jens hair
where sadness takes hold

in the bristles of a brush
and with each stroke
the blinding white light
on nearby headstones
against our windows

become stars in a black sky.

Family Diary
The Farm1919

Part 3
Thursday morning April 17

The cold sun dances
on the ground
and I hear grunts
and know it is father
who does not just work the land,

he loves the land
bleeds in sweat and dirt
in the rows of wheat, corn
in the cold, the heat
in the stench of animal manure

and vomit from hunger and worry
and only stops to drink water
or tell us stories
of when he was a child
and grandfather fought prairie fires

hail, drought and grasshoppers
clouds upon clouds
of fluttering wings
turning the earth dark
leaving a forest of yellow stalks

that in their nakedness,
made grandfather feel naked too.
And then the struggling of plough and horse
cutting through, turning over
and lifting the dirt

as my father leaves me standing
with the wind behind my back
moving farther away
to where the hard prairie
remains untouched.

Steven Pelcman

Family Diary
The Farm 1919

Part 4
Sunday morning May 4

My sister skips through
a field of flowers
near a stream
that snakes its way
across our farm

and she finds herself
in the middle
of a swarm of bees disturbed
and hungry for her
to stop screaming

but she runs until grandfather
covers her with a blanket
and then with vinegar
to ease the pain
and sits up all night

to see if she will die.
She lives
but grandfather is stung too
and days later
thin and unable to speak,

he walks into the woods
slowly with bucket in hand
pretending to pick berries
instead, searching for the right spot
to die.

Family Diary
The Farm 1919

Part 5
Monday morning May 5

We find grandfather
sprawled among dead leaves
and fallen tree limbs
his bucket still in hand
and bring him

to the family cemetery
next to grandma
as Jen plants flowers
and momma watches
from the window

perhaps knowing that only days later,
she will join grandfather
on the day father will cry
staining the wooden casket
he sands down with oil

that mother will lie in,
and baby Jen
will sit on the rocking chair
alone beside the fire
humming herself to sleep.

Steven Pelcman

Family Diary
The Farm 1931

Part 1
Saturday evening June 13

I have always wondered
and dreamed of cities
not far from
death's short walk
where perhaps life

was more than too little
or too much rain,
but as a young man
where my manhood was measured
against the height of corn,

the light of day,
the unspoken word,
in the fields
with horse and plough
buckets of water

every hundred yards
feeling the horse-rein-leather
age in my hands,
I saw my father trying to outrun
the dust bowl clouds

that lifted his shadow
against the dry earth
until he decided to lay
beside my mother and grandfather
in the quiet of family gatherings.

Family Diary
The Farm 1931

Part 2
Sunday morning July 4

On Sunday morning
kneeling against
tombstones
Jen and I pull weeds
from among the rocks

where mother and father
and grandfather lie
among the lined shadows
feathered by butterfly dust
and spiders.

I watch Jen
lose color in her cheeks
from the long days and nights
sitting on mother's rocking chair
with mother's blanket in one hand

tea and whiskey in the other
humming to the movement of dust
the summer swirls of sand
and her baby's play with mice
and rag dolls made of wood and cotton.

Steven Pelcman

Family Diary
The Farm 1932

Part 1
Tuesday September 20

The house smells
of lamp oil and wild roses that
grow beside weathered wood
and I hear my father's
dirt-dried voice

and smell tobacco
on the pages of the same books
that he read to me
I now read to my son
sitting on my lap,

stories of farms, corn
grasshoppers, the wild prairie
and with each turn
of the page
I see my father's pipe sliding

from corner to corner
and feel his touch,
taste the earth,
breathe in leather and lamp oil
and the sweet lilac smells

of mother's hair and the oven bread
aroma on her cheeks in the morning.

Family Diary
The Farm1939

Part 1
Friday night December 22

When I close my eyes
and think of home
I hear the prairie sing
and pull me
to the howling of wolves,

baby Jen's cry
in the middle of the night,
the dust clouds
and the earth
wet with only

my father's sweat
and my mother's sweet humming
in a rocking chair
now kept safe
among the ruins.

They are all gone now:
father, mother, grandfather
and baby Jen.
I feel them within me, always,
as my shovel turns the earth

their hands on mine
in the gentle swaying of
rocking-chair wind
against my face.
If you were to dig deep

into my pockets,
I wish you could pull out
the sweet smell of home.
If only in my head
stars did not burn

with the light of tombstones,
and the prairie
refused to whisper at night.

Touch the Wind
(Normandy, France)

If death
were to take hold
here, among a patchwork
of grassy fields
you would never know
for there is little difference
in the gentle beauty
of such stillness.

It is a cushioned thick earth
full of Gothic stone
and brown-white cows
where white light
fingers its way
through hedgerows
and into the sea

where the blue tide waters
at dusk
still drag skull bones
and bullets to shore
full of windswept shadows
that touch the wind
when a man passes.

Sweet Madeira

Jose's bony fingers and head shake
as he hums and sips sweet Madeira wine
while sitting in the shade of banana trees
stiffened against the humid air
still green late in the season,

but the little glass leaves a syrupy
ring when he pokes his pinky in,
smiles at the dog beneath his feet
and swirls the remaining wine around
his finger and sighs,

"The season is almost over, Nino,"
he mutters to the dog named after his dead son,
all he has left of a life spent on the sea
fishing for scabbard and tuna, drinking with the old men
and washing down the rusty boats as old as he.

His fingers are good for nothing
other than counting the years
and the many times the cable cars
slice through the blue air to rise and drift
to the high hills above

where his wife and daughter and son lie
tucked away in a family patch of dry earth
besides the aroma of sweet Levadas
and cat piss and under the circling buzzards
and encroaching thick clouds.

In another life he might
have been a pirate hugging the coast
and jagged cliffs listening for the sounds
of green canaries and seagulls resisting the wind
or rummaging through the leafy Laurels

stretched across the mountain slopes
where the air may have contained
sugarcane and sweet salt or the dry blood
of African slaves and musket powder
for the killing that always comes with conquering.

Jacaranda and Corals line the alleys
and volcanic hills
and the old wrinkled women
sit on the hot pavement
peddling their handmade shawls and sweaters

their throats too dry to bark,
their eyes too tired to cry
their children too distant to care,
their husbands too dead
to make a difference.

Jose understands that his life
is measured in the long toss of
fishing line glowing silvery
in the moonlight and that one day,
soon, he will sleep

among the Levadas
that carry water and life across
the island leaving his dark shadow
to roam amongst the sea
and sing quiet songs to itself.

Steven Pelcman

A Painting of a Woman

The land is endless at the edge
of the prairie where the town
is small and the church; smaller.

The muted earthly colors
of the mountain-top leans
awkwardly into the lap

of a quarter moon
which finds her angel-lit face
in repose and moths fluttering

on the dried-out empty porch
as her unfinished
words perched

on her lips are surprised
by the darkness
and drift away

into the brush strokes
of fallen stars
and the last breath of light.

She leans against the wooden post
mistaken for the lover
she once was holding onto

all she has and listens
to the tiny voices of children
as crickets break

the silence
of the vast grassland
before her.

Alone among the unyielding
shadows, her fading yellow and green
shawl that she wears is still

prettier than the flowers she must
have planted around a body
of dirt appearing to rise.

Born Again

She is born
on the way to the hospital
in the back seat

of her father's car,
her first breaths inhaling
the lingering stench

of cigarettes and whiskey
and the crumpled
newspaper ads usually tossed

onto the backseat
that her mother's fingers
grasp tightly onto

as the black print
takes hold
while her mother

screams into the corners
of an old Chevy's
dark-red torn leather.

The car races alongside
the old train tracks
that cross Route 81

and had at one time
been a part of a cattle trail
on the edge of prairie

and hasn't lost
the smell of beef and oil
stinking up the Great Plains.

The snow makes the car skid
across the buried wheat
suffering its long silence

any Baptist or old Indian
would understand
as they pass

a dried-out creek
darkened by the outline
of black wings

and trees lost
in the patchwork
of everything else flat

against a crystal sky carrying
only the sounds of an owl
hooting and wood smoke.

In the long winter
land stretches out
into barren fields

full of nothing but flat hard dirt
where nothing grows
in the cold emptiness,

not corn, not flowers, not love,
nothing, as if the mountains
in the distance

don't really exist
other than as a burden
on the land.

How much bigger everything is
bigger than her and the way
light collects darkness

hurling it down at her,
at the farm-house she lives in
as if no one exists

where every day will be
a reminder that life ends here,
that she is lost among the blackness

that fills her world
makes her small,
makes her dreams small.

She will be different
from the loneliness
you get used to on a farm.

She will be more
than the dust and rows of wheat
and learn to see

her parents like hungry animals
in the shadows when as with everything
in darkness, a different truth rises.

She will become a woman
and look out at the prairie
and feel the vibrations of wolves

rather than her father's screams.
How often she will wonder
about the footprints of rabbits

she rarely sees or of the tiny lives
moving freely under the short grass.
How good it will feel to see

the new-born colors
of wild flowers giving hope
to the dry earth.

How much
she will long
for that kind of intimacy.

Steven Pelcman

like water to STONE

The night finds me riding
echoed voices over hills
of accents and howls

that could have scared
any child yet the den couch
did not move an inch

in the winter darkness
and kept the firewood smell
to itself rattling

with the sounds of card chips
and pounding fists
from the basement below.

There was little thought
of memory or of sentiment
for they too

had lives to live
no longer hidden
from the buried light

of where the dead
are waiting
and from the piles

of empty clothing, that SS guards
and cats sniff at,
weighing more than the bony dust

of family members
who never had the chance
to practice their dying

and learn to lie innocently
still with their arms
across their chests.

The world has turned
their nightmares into a glorified
blueprint so that even now

you can see their tattooed numbered
forearms which had once replaced
the need for names or speech

nursing smokestack denials
contradicted by prayer and guilt,
lining up alongside glasses

of scotch shifting and bouncing
with every sudden pounce
against the green circular velvet

as the interrogation lamp
sways above the pot
keeping time with the wind.

There is no sleeping
on these February nights
which like water to stone

the cold ages and penetrates
everything against your skin
leaving the moon

a shadow of itself
and the dark bark of trees
to suffer the silence of snow.

Passchendaele
(First World War -
"The war to end all wars")

For years afterward
trees remained skinless
appearing as dim flashes
of lightning, wobbly and fading
in the water's reflection.

The brown water
of helmets still bob
and the memories
of hunched soldiers;
countless wax figures

in a muddy death,
alongside paths
made of wooden duckboards,
and crushed trees;
solemn bystanders

where the young
are forever young,
now and then rise
to the surface
with the slip of bone

and the gurgling mud
still sloshing through
a hollow skull
where frogs continue
to find refuge.

The marshland grabbed hold of them,
tugged at them from beneath
and pulled them away
from the ant colony of trenches,
from the mustard gas,

the constant bombardments,
the blown-up shell holes,
and out of the heavy rains
only to sink deeply
into the curdling darkness.

They are still there;
shattered voices echoing,
staring at the barbed wire
slithering between the dark
earthy mounds and searching

for the wooden ladders
across the mud and crawling
in the fog and hiding among the
furrows of new born
ploughed earth.

Unknown Faces
(Pogon, Poland 2000)

In Pogon, on a sunny day in August
58 years ago
not far from Auschwitz
my mother was screaming

in front of her home,
when windswept away
to the stomping of feet
on the streets we now walk.

We see a corner brown house
drenched in the summer smell
of ragged lawn blotched
and stained by oil

from a mower in the hands
of a man who smiles at us
with slight shoulders and curved eye
who greets us through a fence

with trembling hands
and whose angular face
leads us into the house
where "the rooms are different,

smaller, dirtier", my mother says,
inching along the corridor
trying not to awaken the dead
stopping once to press her hands

against musty wallpaper
full of printed flowers,
pulling at the edges sticking out
as if peeling skin.

My Bubbie
(Grandmother)

My Bubbie smells
of war-torn Europe and cooked apples.
Thin-lipped and soldier-sure,
her puffed face and dotted eyes hover

over boiling pots of water
and peeled carrots.
Shadows of war cling to her
like skin, as she sits by the small

wooden kitchen table smiling out
the names of brothers and sisters.
She smells of smoldering ash
and brown sugar

and I climb her like a fallen tree,
some limp pile of wood
listening to whispers,
to the voices that bleed from her.

My Bubbie smells of chicken soup
and fresh apricots.
She is my first dinosaur plaything
pet-person, afraid of the dark,

run to, hide to,
all is forgiven place
when I need to be somewhere
safe in the corners of her.

Nine years earlier,
a metal figurehead on the bow
of a ship entering
New York harbor she stood alone

with the taste of salt water
and death in her mouth.
She became all spidery and quiet.
With each visit she would smile

with shiny marble-eyes
push twenty dollars into my hands
walk away, back
to the wooden kitchen

table etched with squiggly lines,
brown and silver smudges
like a war map of Europe
and sit down, waiting.

The Things Little Children Can Do
(Poland 1939)

For a six-year-old to understand death, calmly,
did not surprise her older sister,
who shook her head
and softly croaked out
to her mother and younger brother that
German soldiers were approaching again.

The younger girl whispered
for them to hide in the cellar,
behind the sacks of potatoes
in cold storage
and to not open the door
no matter what.

She closed the front door
behind her
and turned towards the naked body
on the opposite lawn
appearing as a white lump
of dead grass gathered

and left in the rain.
It was not a surprise
for everyone knew he was sick, mad
and no loss to Germans on the hunt,
and it was expected he would share death
with his neighbors that way.

She almost hummed along
as she heard the boots approaching,
noticed the sunlight on them
and did not move
not even when the recoil
of a bullet leaving a gun

found its way into the chest
of the dead neighbor
forcing his shoulders to tremble
the way her lips did
 as she clamoured,
"No Jews here",

and raised her skinny right arm
quickly, as her skirt rose
above her knees,
and then she smiled
with wide eyes and mouth
as if she could be theirs.

The Good Wife

It is a time honored ritual,
feeding a dying husband
baby food in between deep breaths

and stealing kisses
before the next spoonful
finding her instinct,

strength his courage
learns to measure
in cherry-vanilla ice cream.

It is impossible to think
she cannot cheat death,
which should be as effortless

as telling the Rabbi
to reschedule his mourning
or explaining to God

what the concentration camps
had taught her; the art of survival,
in case he has forgotten.

The bedroom windows
reflect her bent trembling
over the hospice bed railing

and above her, outside
everything is black and naked
as it had always been.

Night lights hang shadows
against the walls
and you see things

in an earthly silence, alert
with only the sterilized spinning
of a ceiling fan.

Belonging

The oak tree had been there
next to little farms
and dusty fields
for centuries where donkeys
and Bedouins and camels
passed on the way to Jerusalem.

She kneeled beside the tomatoes
with her face and scooped up
a handful of dirt
with her fingers shaking
and leaned in to the bush
smelling the spiced air.

The sunlight washed away
her wrinkles and puffy cheeks
and grey hair
as her narrow frame
vine like, stretched across
the plants and touched

the dry leaves and short thorns
providing the only shade
an early morning could know.
The booming sound
forced her to look up
her white blouse slipping out

to the shaking tomatoes,
some still half green,
as her knees and elbows
now smudged in dirt
and like a pet,
she felt she belonged there

in a warm spot
comfortable and safe
in the dirt
near the growing and dying
of only tomatoes.
She squinted at the singed line

of imagined birds in the sky
which were rockets arching over clouds
bursting through roofs
on the other side of hills
where little children
were running out of a classroom

of exploding metal and wood
leaving bibles to burn.

Memories of a Child
(1950s New York)

It was war on the streets of New York
in the symphonic whirlwind
of chatter and buses and cabs
driving through the black gas fumes
they left behind.

My father and I follow
in the street-shadowed footsteps
of a Rabbi, whose scraggly beard
and body was designed for stooping
watching him nod

to the bustling crowd
of Saturday street crossers
who pass rows of stands
where blood stained aprons
of sellers bark and buyers

cluck, singular in syllable
and sound, in broken English
and Yiddish, to mimic
the dying voices of hanging
chickens as their drooping bodies

in forgiveness, swirl
above grey barrels full
of sour pickles
and floating onions,
and fish shaking in disbelief

as they are gutted and ribbed,
divided and subdivided into
a chorus line of eyes like lost children
or misplaced buttons
grandmothers save.

Some are still twittering
in their oily golden skin
gasping in their silence,
others flayed white and soggy
and stretched out against ice:

And the flat boxes
of unleavened bread
warming in the summer heat
of Lower East Side New York
like poems, rising out of

the steamy cement
on Orchard street,
where the faces of Europe
in flood cramped tenements,
in buildings lopsided

and unsure of the voices they hear
and it is here, in open store windows
where so many grandfathers
bend over to sell shoes, holding
black stockings with hands that once

held the scaled corpses
of the dying.
They hustle narrow ties and wallets
handkerchiefs and table cloths and
their battered bodies are

like the trade goods they offer;
worn and tossed aside
from the rubble
of pummeled cities
where the dead had piled up

only to be
carted away
in wheelbarrows
like passing trade
at market.

Steven Pelcman

The Confessions of a Dying Man

Enraptured with the odd angle
of oncoming death that stiffens his neck
and beckons his tongue to slither beyond
his dried lips salted by summer heat
he tells a story as quietly as god allows.

Out pours a little mouse-trap
house from his mouth
towering above his childhood
and slanted against Polish streets
carrying horses and buggies

in the shadows of farmers
and old men
wearing yarmulkes
praying in dark corners
to not be seen.

This was his song.
This was his rhythm
as much as his eyelids
now shuddering to lift
his soul away from the

sticky sheets and fleshy smell
of long goodbyes
but he is still bent
on telling us his story
and wets his lips to prepare us.

It was a long time coming
this death of his
and he was ashamed
to have outlived a child
and literally everyone

but this is true of all fathers
and again he wet his lips
with the thoughts of sweet grass
he will lie under
and the coolness of fingers

dipped in the water bowl
before prayers
on Friday evenings
when candle light and rising smoke
transfixed his boyhood.

His eyes burned
and we saw tears.
His fingers gripped the bed
and we saw discolored knuckles
that matched the muted earth

where skinless bones
had been shoveled out
of ovens still warm
and tossed across
dirt fields

where families and whole towns
are buried and in his chin,
the landscape still quivers
with the mere memory
of sisters singing and grandmothers laughing.

All this he expressed, freely
in the bubbled smiles
he managed to release
with the help of an oxygen tank
and morphine needles

that offered salvation
and hope; a deadly cocktail
of Holy Grail ambitions
and wooden crosses
leaning against wailing walls

and you could hear the silent
cries for help and we wondered
if veins would burst
with pain, if muscles
contorted the same way

and if the fatty cysts on his arms
and legs would stop
reminding us of little-crazed
mice scampering
in forgotten mazes

gasping for air,
could come alive
and plead for life
but instead they seemed
to gather and merge

in a gulping motion
when he tried to swallow water.
His narrowed eyes
projected a dim light
too weak to remember

names or faces
other than a wife
who still baited him
with promises of eternity
and desperation

and yet he could not resist
telling us more, knowing
he no longer needed to be
the house-broken pet
rambling in wet diapers

when life was so much easier
being motionless and skinned, scaled
and gutted the way his father
and mother had been
when they were removed

from the face of the earth.
And so you look closely
and wonder how those legs
could have carried so much weight.
How did those arms

not always fall
or was the sound of laughter
different in his head
than how others heard it
and were there voices

that made him forget
himself as if he had never existed,
as if nothing had ever existed
as if every voice was the same voice;
the same endless moment.

There was a grunt, a moan
a second of misunderstood pleasure
before a final cleansing
that saw his body curl up
and nurses panic.

And he turned to one side.
The last turn. The last breath.
The smell of alcohol solution
and body odor, of waste and dead air
and dust piled on window blinds

had no meaning.
They had no meaning.
The darkness could not keep
daylight beyond this room
from taking hold.

He had turned leaving behind
untold stories of when he was young.
He had turned only to have
a terrycloth bathrobe belt latched on
like the good soldier's

helmet strapped tightly beneath the jaw
and chin to keep animal wildness
human and caged. This was the greatest
act of love he could have given;
to make us believe he was confessing

with every word we had said
to ourselves.

Saturday Morning at Temple

Stained glass colored windows
catch sunlight in God's hands
as wet thumbs turn pages

of scripture and the Cantor
sings hymns to the sad rhythmic
swaying of bodies.

Old men and faithful wives
are lined in wooden pews,
and I envision

the deathly innocence of a father
with doll-like beauty
inside the Torah

waiting for the right prayer
as he is gently held
by the Rabbi who walks by

the poetic features of those able to rise,
rising with the weight
of flood and famine

and widows dressed
in flowing skirts and their aloneness
singing high-pitched melodies

and together
a swell of sound
begins to dance

5000 years of history
in their voices
until the final Amen.

Dreamer

She had come from the war-torn
streets of Europe where
the rubble contained
the last images
of the dead.

In the little village near Krakow
she had played with chickens
and fed the hogs
and watched the sun
roll down into the water

of a shallow pond
near her shack
in the early evenings
reflect the dreamy descent
of cranes and herons floating

in a downward arc.
60 years later she remembers
their accidental steps
on legs unprepared
to carry their weight

and tip toe with each
bony stride the way
she does now
as if she carries
our lives on her back.

She stands alone against
the onslaught of clouds
in the narrowing dusk-light
as her stooped back
and rubbery face holds firm

while her squinted eyes
measure out the space on the line
with clothes pins she holds so gently.
One pin is in her mouth
as our laundry hangs and dries

in the wind of our backyard.
It is a ritual of sorts;
her treading ever so carefully
to not walk over
the white sheets and our shirts

draping over her thick arms
and skirting the tall uncut grass.
How proud she must be
of those angels swaying
in the wind with such grace.

About the Author

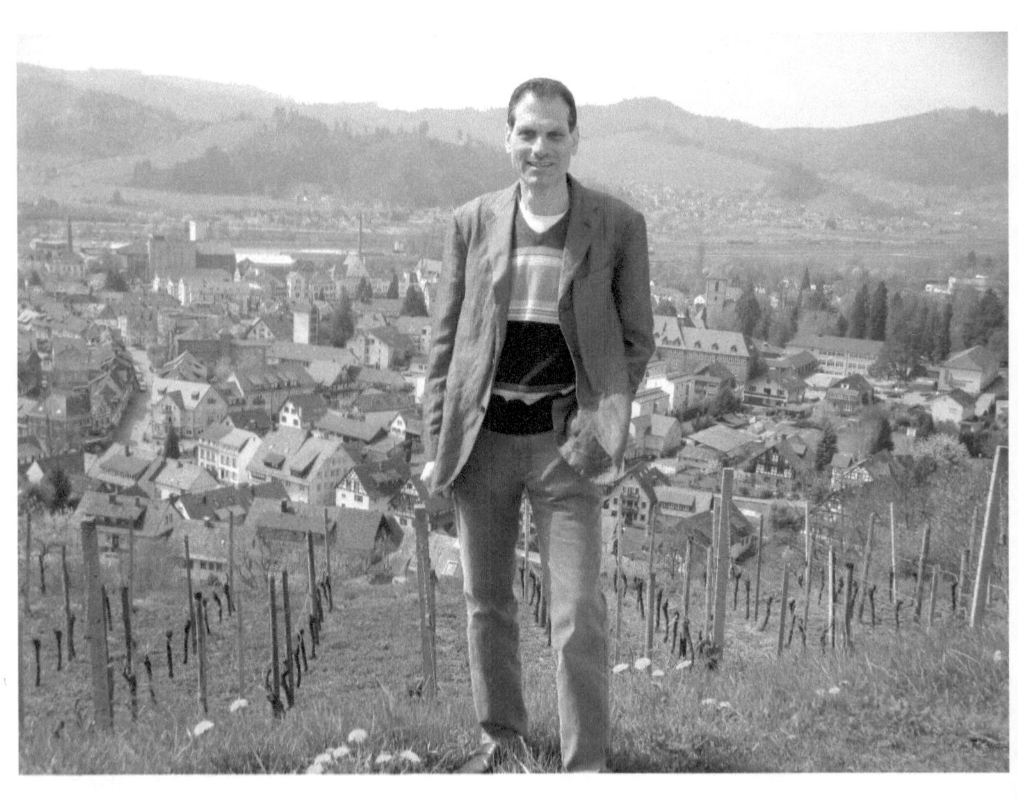

Steven Pelcman is an American educator, film producer and published author who has been residing in Germany for over 19 years. He worked in Hollywood as a producer and reader analyst. Involved as Executive producer in a magazine entertainment program, titled, Yesterdays, a development project which also led him to Washington DC and an invitation to President George H. Bush's inauguration and recognition in the field of TV family programming. Prior to relocating to Germany, Mr. Pelcman, originally from the Bronx, NY had also lived in New Orleans and Los Angeles. He graduated Rockland Community College where he received his AA Degree and SUNY New Paltz where he studied English and literature and graduated in 1976. Mr. Pelcman is now single and his children reside in California.

In Germany, Mr. Pelcman founded a private school, ELT, focusing on teaching English language skills. Eventually this led to a partnership with Siemens throughout Germany. He continues to teach and consult regarding communication skills at the University of Education in Karlsruhe, Germany and at The Baden-Württemberg Cooperative State University, Karlsruhe, Germany and for many schools and corporations in southern Germany. He continues to publish and as recently as 2013, he produced a short film titled, Sugar, based on his own work.

Mr. Pelcman's poetry and short stories have been published in a number of magazines in many countries including the USA, Germany, France, Austria, Israel, Great Britain and others. He has been published in many magazines and journals including: The Windsor Review, The Innisfree Poetry Journal, Fourth River magazine, River Oak Review, Poetry Salzburg Review, Tulane Review, The Baltimore Review, The Warwick Review, The Cape Rock magazine, The Greensboro Review, enskyment.org, Iodine Poetry Journal, Rockhurst Review magazine and many others. He was nominated for the 2012 Pushcart Prize.

Steven Pelcman continues to travel the world, write, publish and teach in an effort to reach readers and share universal experiences, to prepare students of which many will become future teachers and travel to interact with many cultures.

Steven Pelcman says that *"Capturing the voices of humor or pain, making the small moments epic and witnessing the trials and tribulations of the human experience which captures the heart and mind is what drives the work."*

http://stevenpelcman.blogspot.de

Publishing Credits

The author wishes to thank the following publications:

The Greensboro Review USA (A Dying Animal)
Fourth River magazine USA (A Hunter Waits)
Schuylkill Valley Journal USA (A Bat Invades Our
Summer Bungalow)
The Warwick Review England (A Gathering and Saying
Goodbye)
Acta-Victoriana mag Toronto Canada (A Walk with
Miguel)
Rockhurst Review magazine, Rockhurst University USA
(He Needed to Know)
River Oak Review USA (Taos Pueblo)
enskyment.org USA(The Stranger at 3AM, An
Impression)
Poetic Diversity USA (Lake Shrine)
Popshot literary magazine England (A Small World)
The Avalon Literary Review USA (Pool)
Poetry Salzburg Review Austria (Jessica, Andrej,
Acroterion)
Poetrymagazine.com USA (Herbie, Blind, Tuscany, and
published under a different title: Kwa Zulu-Natal South
Africa)
Down in the Dirt Magazine USA (Family Diary,
Thinking, Passchendaele)
The Baltimore Review USA (Between the Lost and the
Forgotten)
Westview magazine -Southwestern Oklahoma State
University USA (Acceptance)
The Windsor Review Canada (The Young Wife, My
Bubbie)
Red Fez USA (Sugar, Home)
Foliate Oak Literary Magazine USA (Saving Frogs,
Falling)
Caffeine magazine USA (First Moment of Custody Visit)

Iodine Poetry Journal USA (At the Window, The Good
Wife)
Voxhumana magazine Israel (Belonging)
Blueline magazine Potsdam State University of New York
USA (Mountain Lake in Fall)
The Cape Rock Magazine USA (Room 229)
Tulane Review USA (Station M8)
Noah Magazine USA (Deer Frozen in Headlights)
Poetica magazine USA (Like Water to Stone)
Innisfree magazine USA (Touch the Wind, Unknown
Faces)
The Jewish Literary Journal USA (The Confessions of a
Dying Man, Saturday Morning at Temple)

www.ingramcontent.com/pod-product-compliance
Lightning Source LLC
Chambersburg PA
CBHW031335060726
47590CB00007B/2484